The Commandments
God's Plan for Our Happy Lives
Reproducible Handouts for Intermediate Grades

Francine M. O'Connor

Active Learning for Catholic Kids
Hi-Time❋Pflaum
Dayton, OH

The Commandments
God's Plan for Our Happy Lives
Reproducible Handouts for Intermediate Grades
Active Learning for Catholic Kids
Francine M. O'Connor

Cover design by Larissa Qvick
Interior design by Patricia Lynch

The Scripture quotations contained herein are from the *New Revised Standard Version of the Bible:* Catholic Edition, ©1993 and 1989 by the Division of Christian Education of the National Council of the Churches of Christ in the U.S.A. All rights reserved. Used by permission.

©2000 Hi-Time✲Pflaum, Dayton, OH 45449. All rights reserved. Photocopying of the material herein is permitted by the publisher for noncommercial use. The permission line must appear on each reproduced page. Any other type of reproduction, transmittal, storage, or retrieval, in any form or by any means, whether electronic or mechanical, including recording, is not permitted without the written consent of the publisher.

ISBN: 0-937997-56-0

Contents

Introduction .... Handing Down the Law
.... Knowing the Rules (2 pages)

First Commandment .... One God Only
.... Other Gods

Second Commandment .... Names of God
.... In the Name of Jesus
.... Learning Respect

Third Commandment .... The Lord's Day
.... Keeping the Lord's Day Holy

Fourth Commandment .... A Reason and a Promise
.... Honor Those Who Care for You

Fifth Commandment .... Choose Life
.... Threats Against Life
.... Dealing with Anger

Sixth Commandment .... Family Loyalty (2 pages)

Seventh Commandment .... The Right Attitude
.... Ways of Stealing

Eighth Commandment .... Telling the Truth
.... From Rumors to Lies

Ninth & Tenth Commandments
.... When Wishes Are Problems

Two Great Commandments .... Love God
.... Love Your Neighbor

Notes to Teacher

Handing Down the Law

Name _____

After the Israelites were freed from slavery in Egypt, they wandered many years in the desert. God stayed with them, and Moses was their leader. Solve this acrostic and learn how God gave Moses a special list of rules for the people to live by. These rules are called the Ten Commandments.

Clues

1. Time of darkness $\overline{35}\ \overline{9}\ \overline{4}\ \overline{27}\ \overline{17}$

2. Place of God's kingdom $\overline{8}\ \overline{21}\ \overline{34}\ \overline{6}\ \overline{28}\ \overline{33}$

3. A party favor filled with air $\overline{19}\ \overline{5}\ \overline{20}\ \overline{20}\ \overline{30}\ \overline{16}\ \overline{35}$

4. To run after someone $\overline{29}\ \overline{8}\ \overline{18}\ \overline{23}\ \overline{13}$

5. Funny person with a red nose $\overline{29}\ \overline{20}\ \overline{2}\ \overline{15}\ \overline{33}$

6. Place where bees make honey $\overline{12}\ \overline{9}\ \overline{31}\ \overline{32}$

7. Used for biting and chewing $\overline{22}\ \overline{32}\ \overline{7}\ \overline{36}\ \overline{12}$

8. Glove worn by a catcher $\overline{10}\ \overline{9}\ \overline{14}\ \overline{11}$

9. Opposite of slow $\overline{25}\ \overline{18}\ \overline{23}\ \overline{26}$

10. A precious metal $\overline{1}\ \overline{24}\ \overline{20}\ \overline{3}$

$\overline{1}\ \overline{2}\ \overline{3}\ \ \overline{4}\ \overline{5}\ \overline{6}\ \overline{7}\ \ \overline{8}\ \overline{9}\ \overline{10}$

$\overline{11}\ \overline{12}\ \overline{13}\ \ \overline{14}\ \overline{15}\ \overline{16}$

$\overline{17}\ \overline{18}\ \overline{19}\ \overline{20}\ \overline{21}\ \overline{22}\ \overline{23}\ \ \overline{24}\ \overline{25}$

$\overline{26}\ \overline{27}\ \overline{28}\ \ \overline{29}\ \overline{30}\ \overline{31}\ \overline{32}\ \overline{33}\ \overline{34}\ \overline{35}\ \overline{36}$.

©2000 Hi-Time✦Pflaum, Dayton, OH 45449 (800-543-4383). Permission is granted by the publisher to reproduce this page for classroom use only.

Knowing the Rules

Name _____

TEN COMMANDMENTS

1. I am the Lord, your God. You shall not have strange gods before me.
2. You shall not take the name of the Lord your God in vain.
3. Remember to keep holy the Lord's day.
4. Honor your father and your mother.
5. You shall not kill.
6. You shall not commit adultery.
7. You shall not steal.
8. You shall not bear false witness against your neighbor.
9. You shall not covet your neighbor's wife.
10. You shall not covet your neighbor's goods.

After reading each situation, write which commandment it involves and why.

Marina and Joyce were good friends. When Joyce turned 13, her mother gave her a ring that had been her grandmother's. Joyce wore the ring to school and everyone thought it was beautiful and very special. Marina wished she had a special ring too, and decided that Joyce was just showing off. By the end of the day, Marina refused to even speak to Joyce.

_____
_____
_____

Rafael loves sports. Every evening and all weekend, he is either practicing, playing, or watching some kind of sport. Because sports are so important to him, he rarely pays attention to anything or anybody else—especially God.

_____
_____
_____

Sharon and Tanya were on their way to Sunday Mass. They had to pass the mall and decided to do an hour's worth of shopping instead.

_____
_____
_____

©2000 Hi-Time◆Pflaum, Dayton, OH 45449 (800-543-4383). Permission is granted by the publisher to reproduce this page for classroom use only.

Knowing the Rules
(page 2)

Name _____

Louis and Terrence stayed after school to watch a soccer game. When the game ended, Terrence's dad came to get them. "Wow, neat car!" Louis said, when he saw Terrence's dad drive up in a brand new SUV. "Yeah, it's great. My dad's company had a good year, so he got a nice bonus." "My dad's too stupid to earn a lot of money," said Louis. "We'll be driving around in our old station wagon forever."

_____
_____
_____

Chris was walking through the hall between classes one day. All of a sudden, out of nowhere, somebody bumped into Chris and books flew. "Oops, sorry about that," said the other student as she hurried off. Chris was so angry that instead of accepting the apology, Chris made an offensive gesture toward the girl.

_____
_____
_____

Michael was broke, but he was browsing through the CD selections at the music store anyway. He found one he *really* wanted. When no one was looking, he slipped it under his jacket.

_____
_____
_____

One evening, Terry's little brother got into Terry's baseball card collection and ruined five of the best cards. Terry yelled at his brother and hit him so hard on the arm that he got a big bruise.

_____
_____
_____

One Friday night, Maria was at a friend's house, and her friend wanted to watch an X-rated movie. Maria knew that seeing an X-rated movie was not what she should do. After thinking about it for a few seconds, Maria said, "Sure, no problem."

_____
_____
_____

Talisha lived across the street from Maurice, who was always teasing her. One trash day, someone pushed all the trash cans into the street and dumped their contents all over the neighborhood. Talisha didn't know who did it, but she told everyone that Maurice did it so that he'd get in trouble.

_____
_____
_____

At first, Colin only cursed when he got angry, but after awhile he got so used to it that he didn't even have to be angry to curse. His coach talked to Colin about his bad habit but Colin just walked away thinking, "It's no big deal. I'm not hurting anybody."

_____
_____
_____

©2000 Hi-Time*Pflaum, Dayton, OH 45449 (800-543-4383). Permission is granted by the publisher to reproduce this page for classroom use only.

One God Only

Name _____

The first commandment says: "I am the Lord, your God. You shall not have strange gods before me." This means that God has a special relationship with us. God is not some being living far out of our sight. Our God knows us and loves us. Decode this message to discover the special promise God makes to all who believe and obey.

Key

A = E	H = I	O = D
B = F	I = T	Q = S
C = Y	J = U	V = H
D = R	L = K	W = A
E = M	M = N	X = L
F = P	N = G	Z = B
G = O		

"___ ___ ___   ___ ___ ___ ___   ___ ___   ___ ___ ___
 C G J   Q V W X X   Z A   B G D

___ ___ ___   ___ ___ ___ ___ ___ ___
 E A W   F D H A Q I X C

___ ___ ___ ___ ___ ___   ___ ___ ___ ___   ___ ___ ___ ___
 L H M N O G E   W M O W   V G X C

___ ___ ___ ___ ___."
 M W I H G M

(Exodus 19:6)

You shall not make for yourself an idol...

©2000 Hi-Time▪Pflaum, Dayton, OH 45449 (800-543-4383). Permission is granted by the publisher to reproduce this page for classroom use only.

Other Gods

Name _____

Anything that gets in the way of our love, honor, and worship of God becomes another god in our lives. For example, if we place more importance on winning awards than we do on loving God, we have created another god to honor. If our desire to get high grades causes us to cheat, we have created another god to obey. If we miss Mass to go to a game, we have created another god to worship. If we think more about being popular with our friends than with God, we have created other gods to love.

Below is a list of things that may (or may not) become other gods for us. These things are not bad in themselves, but they can be dangerous if we place too much importance on them. Find and circle each of these things in the puzzle.

```
D Q G A M E S E D H
R T O Y S J S K G O
U R T I X A U O C C
G B A S E B A L L K
S R M P C N G I O E
P O P U L A R I T Y
M O N E Y O A L H J
F K A W A R D S E G
W Z C E H D E Y S V
C P O W E R S M H B
```

Word List

AWARDS	CLOTHES	GAMES
HOCKEY	POPULARITY	PRAISE
BASEBALL	DRUGS	GRADES
MONEY	POWER	TOYS

©2000 Hi-Time❖Pflaum, Dayton, OH 45449 (800-543-4383). Permission is granted by the publisher to reproduce this page for classroom use only.

Names of God

Name _____

A long time ago, people would not even say the name of God out loud. They knew how holy God's name was and did not want to misuse it in any way. Whenever we say that sacred name, we call upon all of God's power and love to be with us.

Jesus gave us several names by which we can call God. Others we have learned from our prayers. Some of these names are scrambled below.

HEAFTR
_ _ _ _ _ _

RECAORT
_ _ _ _ _ _ _

ABAB
_ _ _ _

STAMRE
_ _ _ _ _ _

HET YGHITMLA
_ _ _ _ _ _ _ _ _ _ _

VENHAEYL GNKI
_ _ _ _ _ _ _ _ _ _ _

WHHYAE
_ _ _ _ _ _

Can you think of any other names for God?

In the Name of Jesus

Name _____

Jesus is God's Son, the second Person of the Holy Trinity. The second commandment also commands us not to use the name of Jesus except in prayer. Solve this puzzle to find how Saint Paul referred to the name of Jesus in Philippians 2:9.

1. The opposite of far

   ___ ___ ___ ___
   4   15 24 22

2. Someone between the ages of twelve and twenty

   ___ ___ ___ ___
   1   21 12 23

3. Another name for God's kingdom

   ___ ___ ___ ___ ___ ___
   20 26 5   14 7   4

4. Someone who casts a ballot

   ___ ___ ___ ___ ___
   11 18 19 3   16

5. Not a girl

   ___ ___ ___
   9   10 17

6. Everyone has one

   ___ ___ ___ ___
   23 8   6   13

7. The place where a family lives

   ___ ___ ___ ___
   2   18 25 3

"___ ___ ___
 1   2   3

___ ___ ___ ___
4   5   6   7

___ ___ ___ ___ ___
8   9   10 11 12

___ ___ ___ ___ ___
13 14 15 16 17

___ ___ ___ ___ ___
18 19 20 21 22

___ ___ ___ ___.''
23 24 25 26

©2000 Hi-Time❋Pflaum, Dayton, OH 45449 (800-543-4383). Permission is granted by the publisher to reproduce this page for classroom use only.

Learning Respect

Name _____

Obeying the second commandment is simply a matter of learning to love and respect God. Solve this puzzle to learn what Paul says we should do when we hear Jesus' name. (See Philippians 2:10,11.)

"_A_ _T_ _T_ _H_ _E_ _N_ _A_ _M_ _E_ _O_ _F_ _J_ _E_ _S_ _U_ _S_

_E_ _V_ _E_ _R_ _Y_ _K_ _N_ _E_ _E_ _S_ _H_ _O_ _U_ _L_ _D_ _B_ _E_ _N_ _D_,

_I_ _N_ _H_ _E_ _A_ _V_ _E_ _N_ _A_ _N_ _D_ _O_ _N_ _E_ _A_ _R_ _T_ _H_

_A_ _N_ _D_ _U_ _N_ _D_ _E_ _R_ _T_ _H_ _E_ _E_ _A_ _R_ _T_ _H_,

_A_ _N_ _D_ _E_ _V_ _E_ _R_ _Y_ _T_ _O_ _N_ _G_ _U_ _E_

_S_ _H_ _O_ _U_ _L_ _D_ _C_ _O_ _N_ _F_ _E_ _S_ _S_ _T_ _H_ _A_ _T_

_J_ _E_ _S_ _U_ _S_ _C_ _H_ _R_ _I_ _S_ _T_ _I_ _S_ _L_ _O_ _R_ _D_."

Code

=A	=G	=N	=U
=B	=H	=O	=V
=C	=I	=P	=W
=D	=J	=Q	=X
=E	=K	=R	=Y
=F	=L	=S	=Z
	=M	=T	

©2000 Hi-Time·Pflaum, Dayton, OH 45449 (800-543-4383). Permission is granted by the publisher to reproduce this page for classroom use only.

The Lord's Day

Name _____

Long ago, before Jesus was born, the Hebrew rulers had a long list of strict laws about how the people were to keep the Lord's day holy. They could not cook their meals, sweep the floor, work in the fields, or even walk down the street to visit a neighbor on the Sabbath. This made it very difficult for people to keep the law. And the penalties for disobeying the law were tough.

When Jesus came, he saw a need to change that. In Mark 2:23-28, we read that one day he was walking through a grain field with his disciples. Some of the disciples reached down and plucked the heads from the grain to eat. This shocked some who saw them. "Look, why are they doing what is not lawful on the Sabbath?" they asked. Solve the acrostic to see what Jesus told them.

1. Something you eat with jam or butter — B R E A D (6, 20, 3, 12, 23)
2. What you write on — P A P E R (25, 5, 28, 17, 20)
3. Green stuff on your lawn — G R A S S (21, 20, 15, 13, 24)
4. Melt, unfreeze — T H A W (1, 10, 8, 11)
5. An explosive device — B O M B (7, 19, 14, 6)
6. Fruit, vegetables, meat, etc. — F O O D (18, 22, 27, 16)
7. A lead for your dog — L E A S H (29, 26, 5, 4, 2)
8. An exam — T E S T (9, 30, 4, 1)

"T H E   S A B B A T H   W A S   M A D E   F O R   G O D'S   P E O P L E."

Keeping the Lord's Day Holy

Name _____

God set aside one day out of each week for us to rest from our labors, to spend extra time with God, and to enjoy the world made especially for us.

What does your family do on the Lord's day? These four pictures show some ways families celebrate the Lord's day. Below them are four quotes from Scripture that help to fit each Sunday to God's Word. Study each picture, then number it according to the quote that fits it best.

☐ We Worship Together.

☐ We Visit the Sick.

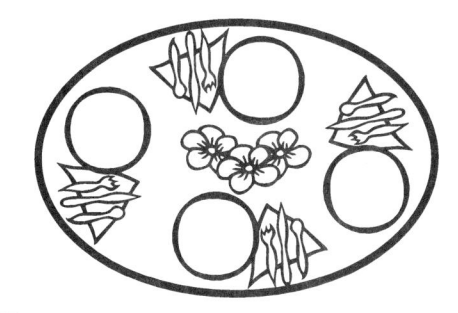

☐ We Share a Family Meal.

☐ We Go for a Praise Walk.

1. "Come, therefore, let us enjoy the good things that exist, and make use of the creation to the full" (Wisdom 2:6).

2. "They broke bread at home and ate their food with glad and generous hearts, praising God and having the goodwill of all the people" (Acts 2:46-47).

3. "Do this in remembrance of me" (Luke 22:19).

4. "Do not hesitate to visit the sick, because for such deeds you will be loved" (Sirach 7:35).

Add your own ideas for keeping the Lord's day holy.

_____

_____

_____

©2000 Hi-Time❋Pflaum, Dayton, OH 45449 (800-543-4383). Permission is granted by the publisher to reproduce this page for classroom use only.

A Reason and a Promise

Name _____

God knows that young people need someone to guide them, to teach them, and to love and care for them. The fourth commandment requires you to honor and respect your parents and those who watch over you. This commandment is so important that God included a reason to obey, and gave a wonderful promise. To discover the reason and the promise, solve the circle quote by reading every other letter around the circle.

Start here. ▸

Circle letters: S D O Y T O H U A M T A I Y T L M I A V V E B L E O W N E G L O L N W T I H T E H E Y A O R U T A H N

" _ _ _ _ _ _ _ _ _ _ _ _ _ _ _ _

_ _ _ _ _ _ _ _ _ _ _ _ _

_ _ _ _ _ _ _ _ _ _ _ _ _ _ _ _ _ _."

(Ephesians 6:3)

©2000 HI-Time❋Pflaum, Dayton, OH 45449 (800-543-4383). Permission is granted by the publisher to reproduce this page for classroom use only.

Honor Those Who Care for You

Name _____

Instead of waiting for a special day every year to honor your mother or father or others who care for you, you can take advantage of everyday opportunities. To make a coupon book of promises, you will need seven 3" X 5" index cards, glue or paste, and a stapler. On each index card, paste one of the six promises cut from this page. Make the cover for the book with the extra card. Staple the cards together along the left side so the coupons can be removed one at a time.

PROMISE COUPON BOOK

To:

From:

Promise Coupon

Coupon holder to receive breakfast in bed on one Saturday.

Redeem within six months.

Promise Coupon

Coupon holder to receive one (1) sweeping of the garage.

Redeem within six months.

Promise Coupon

This coupon entitles the bearer to four (4) hours help in the yard on a weekend agreeable to both of us.

Redeem within six months.

Promise Coupon

Coupon good for one (1) car wash and one (1) vacuuming of inside of car.

Redeem within six months.

Promise Coupon

This coupon entitles the bearer to unlimited hugs from me.

No expiration.

Promise Coupon

Redeem this coupon for one (1) free cup of tea or comparable beverage made by me and served with a smile.

Renewable at donor's discretion.

©2000 Hi-Time✠Pflaum, Dayton, OH 45449 (800-543-4383). Permission is granted by the publisher to reproduce this page for classroom use only.

Choose Life

Name _____

Life is our most precious gift from God. The fifth commandment tells us that we must respect and protect this gift in all its forms. From the time we are conceived until the moment that we die, God is watching over us and protecting our lives. Every life is important to God and only God can choose when a life on earth is ended. There was a great man, Cardinal Joseph Bernardin, who first used a phrase that stands for respecting life from conception to death. Decode the puzzle to discover this phrase.

Code

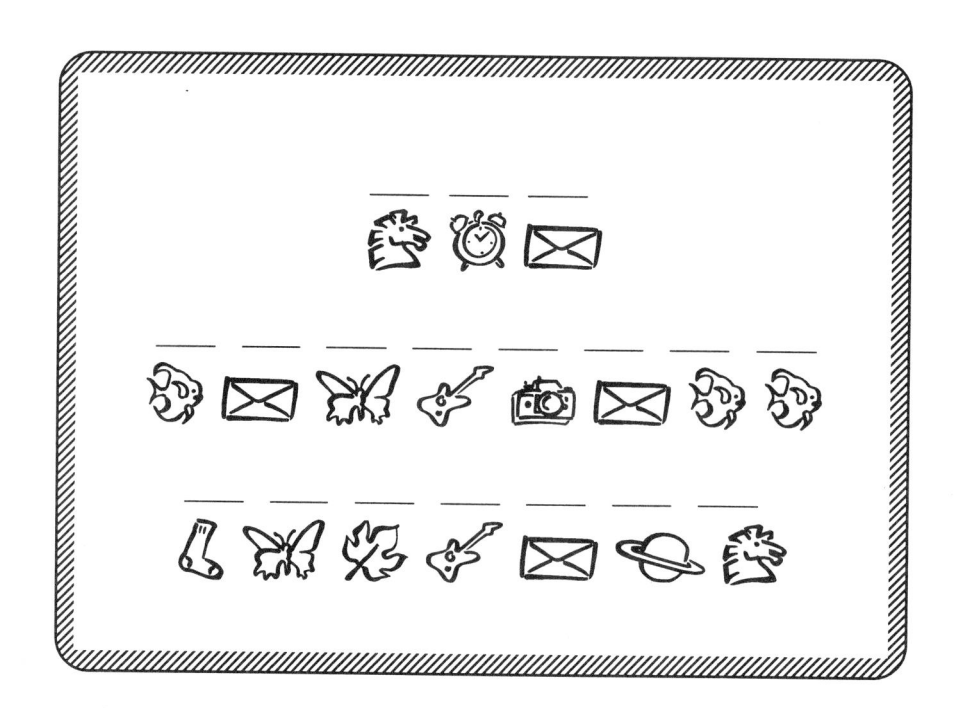

butterfly =A, sock =G, planet =N, knife =U
sun =B, clock =H, glasses =O, cloud =V
clover =C, hand =I, column =P, apple =W
shell =D, boot =J, tree =Q, strawberry =X
envelope =E, car =K, leaf =R, cup =Y
heart =F, camera =L, lion =S, key =Z
guitar =M, unicorn =T

___ ___ ___
 T   H   E

___ ___ ___ ___ ___ ___ ___ ___
 S   E   A   M   L   E   S   S

___ ___ ___ ___ ___ ___ ___ ___
 G   A   R   M   E   N   T

To discover where Cardinal Bernardin found this phrase, look at John 19:23. What does the phrase refer to? Write your answer here.

_____

_____

_____

_____

Threats Against Life

Name _____

Unfortunately, some people believe that killing is acceptable under certain conditions. Christians must always object to the tendency to make killing acceptable or legal. Finish the following sentences using words from the Word List, then circle those killings that are legal in this country. (Remember, legal does not always make it right in God's eyes.)

Word List

- mercy killing
- suicide
- manslaughter
- murder
- abortion
- electric chair
- gas chamber
- euthanasia
- execution
- lethal injection

1. Taking the life of the unborn is called __ __ __ __ __ __ __ __ .

2. Enforcing the death penalty means taking a life through some means of __ __ __ __ __ __ __ __ __ .

3. In some areas, the death penalty is carried out by putting people to death in the __ __ __ __ __ __ __ __ __ __ __ .

4. Taking a life in anger is sometimes called __ __ __ __ __ __ __ __ __ __ __ .

5. Another method used for carrying out a death sentence is the __ __ __ __ __ __ __ __ __ __ __ .

6. Taking the life of a person who is suffering is called __ __ __ __ __ __ __ __ __ __ __ .

7. Another term used for taking the life of a sick person is __ __ __ __ __ __ __ __ __ __ __ __ __ .

8. Intentionally taking someone else's life is called __ __ __ __ __ __ .

9. Taking one's own life is called __ __ __ __ __ __ __ .

10. Some believe that enforcing the death penalty through __ __ __ __ __ __ __ __ __ __ __ __ __ __ __ is more "humane" than other methods.

©2000 Hi-Time✻Pflaum, Dayton, OH 45449 (800-543-4383). Permission is granted by the publisher to reproduce this page for classroom use only.

Dealing with Anger

Name _____

While most of us would never intentionally kill another person, there are other kinds of killing. We can kill a friendship with anger. We can kill a person's self-esteem with insults. We can hurt a person's feelings when we call that person names. Like every other commandment, the fifth commandment is a commandment of love. Jesus said, "If you are angry with a brother or sister, you will be liable to judgment" (Matthew 5:22).

There are things we can do when we feel angry. We can pray for God to take away our anger. We can talk to the person with whom we are angry and try to settle our differences. We can do something loving for the person with whom we are angry. We can remember all the nice things we know about that person.

1 Think of one person with whom you've ever been angry. Write down a code word for the person. (Example: if the person plays soccer, make your code word "Sweeper.")

_____

2 Describe how you felt when you were angry.

_____
_____
_____

3 What did you do about your anger?

_____
_____
_____

4 What do you think Jesus would have told you to do?

_____
_____
_____

5 Name three things you do to get over being angry with someone.

_____
_____
_____

©2000 Hi-Time❋Pflaum, Dayton, OH 45449 (800-543-4383). Permission is granted by the publisher to reproduce this page for classroom use only.

Family Loyalty

Marriage is God's plan for creating a strong and healthy family in which children can grow up. Love and loyalty within the family strengthen the family unit. God gave us the sixth commandment to protect the relationship between husband and wife, which in turn helps protect every relationship within the family.

Name _____

Using the tree pattern on page 2, create your own family tree. Fill in the names of your family members on this page, cut around them, and paste them on the tree. Use the extra spots if you need them. You may need the help of your family to complete this project.

My Mother's Mother	My Mother's Father	My Father's Mother
My Father's Father	My Mother	My Father
My Sister	My Sister	My Sister
My Brother	My Brother	My Brother
My _____	My _____	My _____
My _____	My _____	My _____

©2000 Hi-Time✴Pflaum, Dayton, OH 45449 (800-543-4383). Permission is granted by the publisher to reproduce this page for classroom use only.

Family Loyalty
(page 2)

Name _____

The _____ Family Tree

The Right Attitude

Name _____

The seventh commandment is all about a special attitude toward others. It means we care enough about others to never take away something that belongs to them. It means we would never do anything to harm their possessions. It means treating the possessions of others as we would treat our own possessions. Solve the rebus to see what this attitude is.

[rebus puzzle]

_ _ _ _ _ _ _

The Story of Zacchaeus

To learn more about this attitude, read the story of Zacchaeus in Luke 19:1-10. Then answer these questions.

1. Zacchaeus was a _____.

   This job enabled him to cheat many people.

2. In order to see Jesus, Zacchaeus had to _____ _____.

3. Jesus tells Zacchaeus he wants to _____ _____.

4. What two things will Zacchaeus do to show he has changed his attitude toward others?

   _____
   _____

Ways of Stealing

Name _____

There are many ways to break the commandment against stealing. We can steal other people's physical property, copy their homework, destroy or tear up something belonging to them, hide something that belongs to them; or we can borrow and then lose someone else's possession and not pay to replace it. Using the Word List, see how many ways of stealing you find in the hidden-word square.

Word List
ABUSE
COPY
DESTROY
HIDE
LOSE
SHOPLIFT
STEAL
TEAR UP
VANDALIZE

And all these actions show a lack of
RESPECT

```
A  S  H  O  P  L  I  F  T  B
E  T  I  N  R  C  S  O  J  F
W  E  X  B  G  I  H  D  Y  U
V  A  N  D  A  L  I  Z  E  T
H  L  K  O  B  S  D  T  P  L
M  Q  U  W  U  V  E  R  N  F
Z  A  R  E  S  P  E  C  T  O
P  T  E  U  E  Q  L  O  S  E
G  K  T  E  A  R  U  P  M  H
C  D  E  S  T  R  O  Y  L  D
```

©2000 Hi-Time❖Pflaum, Dayton, OH 45449 (800-543-4383). Permission is granted by the publisher to reproduce this page for classroom use only.

Telling the Truth

Name _____

To "bear false witness" means to tell lies or spread rumors that are not true. The eighth commandment is about the value of truth. In a quote from Ephesians (4:15a), Paul tells us what happens when we speak the truth. Solve the acrostic to see what Paul says.

1. Use water colors ___ ___ ___ ___ ___
   34 4 52 36 28

2. The color of grass ___ ___ ___ ___ ___
   29 40 24 11 36

3. The very top of a mountain ___ ___ ___ ___
   2 22 43 5

4. Working in stitches ___ ___ ___ ___ ___ ___
   27 39 42 6 46 8

5. Two halves ___ ___ ___ ___ ___
   32 10 20 19 37

6. What this commandment is about ___ ___ ___ ___ ___
   28 30 33 47 50

7. A doctor's helper ___ ___ ___ ___ ___
   7 26 51 1 3

8. A building where we pray together ___ ___ ___ ___ ___ ___
   49 16 14 13 49 10

9. Tiny purple flower ___ ___ ___ ___ ___ ___
   21 17 31 19 3 12

10. Like the prickly stem of a rose ___ ___ ___ ___ ___ ___
    54 10 48 30 46 44

11. Very, very small ___ ___ ___ ___
    9 35 18 41

12. A, E, I, O, and U ___ ___ ___ ___ ___ ___
    38 31 42 3 19 53

13. A flat one on a car is a problem ___ ___ ___ ___
    15 45 30 37

14. A cat's cry ___ ___ ___ ___
    25 3 31 23

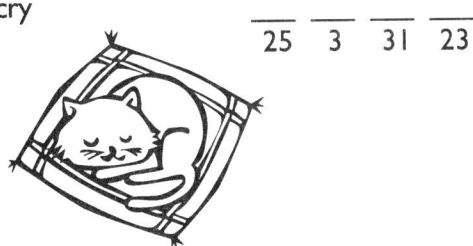

"___ ___ ___ ___ ___ ___ ___ ___ ___ ___ ___ ___ ___ ___ ___ ___ ___ ___
  1 2 3 4 5 6 7 8   9 10 11 12 13 14 15 16 17 18

___ ___ ___ ___ ___ ___ ___ ___ ___ ___ ___ ___ ___ ___ ___ ___ ___ ___
19 20 21 22 23 24 25 26 27 28 29 30 31 32 33 34 35 36

___ ___ ___ ___ ___ ___ ___ ___ ___ ___ ___ ___ ___ ___ ___ ___ ___ ___."
37 38 39 40 41 42 43 44 45 46 47 48 49 50 51 52 53 54

©2000 Hi-Time❋Pflaum, Dayton, OH 45449 (800-543-4383). Permission is granted by the publisher to reproduce this page for classroom use only.

From Rumors to Lies

Name _____

Remember the game called "Telephone"? The players sit in a circle, and the first player whispers something into the second player's ear. Then the second player whispers into the third player's ear, and so on. Most often, the words that the last person speaks are nothing like the words that the first person spoke. It's a good example of how rumors can become lies, and why spreading gossip or rumors of any kind can be dangerous.

Here is a word game called "Changelings" that demonstrates how a word's entire meaning can change by changing just one letter in it. And each time another letter changes, the word gets even further from its true meaning. Using the clues, see how you can change WORDS into HARMS by changing only one letter in the previous word.

We find many of these in the dictionary.   W O R D S

Small wiggly creatures often used for bait.   _ _ _ _ _

In the winter, the fire does this for us.   _ _ _ _ _

In the country, you see many of these.   _ _ _ _ _

Every rumor we spread about someone does this.   H A R M S

Now see if you can change LOVE into HATE and then back into LOVE.

What we should feel toward God and neighbor   L O V E

The ____ Ranger   _ _ _ _

A path or small road   _ _ _ _

Not on time   _ _ _ _

The opposite of love   H A T E

Destiny   _ _ _ _

What we pay when we ride a bus or cab   _ _ _ _

A piece of merchandise   _ _ _ _

How a furnace keeps our homes   _ _ _ _

A patient might be in one in a hospital   _ _ _ _

Another word for grease used in cooking   _ _ _ _

One of God's titles   _ _ _ _

The Bible is the _____ of God.   _ _ _ _

Yesterday, the player _____ a helmet on his head.   _ _ _ _

She _____ her hair into braids.   _ _ _ _

The opposite of hate   L O V E

©2000 Hi-Time❊Pflaum, Dayton, OH 45449 (800-543-4383). Permission is granted by the publisher to reproduce this page for classroom use only.

When Wishes Are Problems

Name _____

We all make wishes. We all have hopes and dreams. Wishes, hopes, and dreams are all good things. But they can become bad things if we allow ourselves to wish, hope, and dream for someone or something that belongs to someone else. To covet means to be so jealous that we wish harm would come to the person we envy, or we want to do harm to that person ourselves. Instead of being happy for our neighbor's good fortune, we feel resentment—possibly even hate. These feelings do terrible things to us and to our relationships with others. Friendship dies. Kindness dies. Love dies. Below are five things to do to avoid being covetous.

1 Write a short prayer asking God to help you overcome your feelings of jealousy and envy.

_____
_____
_____
_____

2 Write a special love-prayer for someone who has something you want.

_____
_____
_____
_____

3 List three good things God has given you.   _____ _____ _____

4 Write a letter thanking God for being so good to you.

DEAR GOD,

5 Name three friends with whom you can share your blessings.

_____
_____
_____

©2000 Hi-Time*Pflaum, Dayton, OH 45449 (800-543-4383). Permission is granted by the publisher to reproduce this page for classroom use only.

Love God

Name _____

Jesus gave us two great commandments of love. If you faithfully follow Jesus' two commandments, you will never break even one of the Ten Commandments. Solve the coded message to discover the first of Jesus' commandments. After you have solved the puzzle, answer the question below the quote.

"_____ _____ _____ _____ _____
_____ _____ _____ _____ _____
_____, _____ _____ _____ _____,
_____ _____ _____ _____, _____
_____ _____ _____ _____."

(Mark 12:30)

Code

=A	=G	=N	=U
=B	=H	=O	=V
=C	=I	=P	=W
=D	=J	=Q	=X
=E	=K	=R	=Y
=F	=L	=S	=Z
	=M	=T	

Which three of the Ten Commandments do we keep by following Jesus' first commandment?

_____

_____

_____

©2000 Hi-Time•Pflaum, Dayton, OH 45449 (800-543-4383). Permission is granted by the publisher to reproduce this page for classroom use only.

Love Your Neighbor

Name _____

Someone once asked Jesus, "Who is my neighbor?" Jesus answered with the story of the Good Samaritan. Read Luke 10:25-37, then solve the crossword to find out who your neighbors are.

Across

1. This neighbor keeps you safe.
4. This neighbor drives you to school in a big yellow vehicle.
5. This neighbor responds to fires and other emergency calls.
8. This neighbor takes care of you every day.
10. This neighbor helps the doctor keep you healthy.
11. This neighbor is a mother or father to your mother or father.
12. This neighbor plays with you every day.

Down

2. This neighbor helps you across the street after school.
3. This neighbor brings letters and cards to your house.
6. This neighbor helps you to learn.
7. This neighbor probably sits right next to you in school.
9. This neighbor keeps you healthy.

©2000 Hi-Time•Pflaum, Dayton, OH 45449 (800-543-4383). Permission is granted by the publisher to reproduce this page for classroom use only.

Notes to Teacher

Handing Down the Law
Clues: night; heaven; balloon; chase; clown; hive; teeth; mitt; fast; gold
Answer: God gave him the two tablets of the covenant.

Knowing the Rules
Note: This exercise provides excellent discussion starters for a class or for a small group activity.

One God Only
Answer: "You shall be for me a priestly kingdom and a holy nation" (Exodus 19:6).

Other Gods

```
D Q G A M E S E D H
R T O Y S J S K G O
U R T I X A U O C U
G B A S E B A L L K
S R M P C N G I O E
P O P U L A R I T Y
M O N E Y O A L H J
F K A W A R D S E G
W Z C E H D E Y S V
C P O W E R S M H B
```

Names of God
Father; Abba; The Almighty; Creator; Master; Heavenly King; Yahweh

In the Name of Jesus
Clues: near; teen; heaven; voter; boy; name; home
Answer: The name above every other name.

Learning Respect
"At the name of Jesus every knee should bend, in heaven and on earth and under the earth, and every tongue should confess that Jesus Christ is Lord" (Philippians 2:10,11).

The Lord's Day
Clues: bread; paper; grass; thaw; bomb; food; leash; test
Answer: The Sabbath was made for God's people.

A Reason and a Promise
"So that it may be well with you and you may live long on the earth" (Ephesians 6:1).

Choose Life
Answer: The Seamless Garment

Threats Against Life
Answers: 1=abortion; 2=execution; 3=electric chair; 4=manslaughter; 5=gas chamber; 6=euthanasia; 7=mercy killing; 8=murder; 9=suicide; 10=lethal injection.
Legal (depending on state or national laws): abortion; execution; electric chair; gas chamber; lethal injection.

The Right Attitude
[reel]-[eel]+[vest]-v+[ape]-[tape]+m+[pail]-[mail]+[neck]-n-k+[tear]-[ear] = Respect

Ways of Stealing

```
A S H O P L I F T B
E T I N R C S O J F
W E X B G I H D Y U
V A N D A L I Z E T
H L K O B S D T P L
M Q U W U V E R N F
Z A R E S P E C T O
P T E U E Q L O S E
G K T E A R U P M H
C D E S T R O Y L D
```

Telling the Truth
Answers to clues: 1=paint; 2=green; 3=peak; 4=sewing; 5=whole; 6=truth; 7=nurse; 8=church; 9=violet; 10=thorny; 11=tiny; 12=vowels; 13=tire; 14=meow.

Answer to acrostic: "Speaking the truth in love, we must grow up in every way into Christ."

From Rumors to Lies
Answers to first exercise: words; worms; warms; farms; harms
Answers to second exercise: love; lone; lane; late; hate; fate; fare; ware; warm; ward; lard; lord; word; wore; wove; love

Love God
Answer: "You shall love the Lord your God with all your heart, with all your soul, with all your mind, and with all your strength" (Mark 12:30).

Love Your Neighbor
Across: 1=police officer; 4=bus driver; 5=firefighter; 8=parent; 10=nurse; 11=grandparent; 12=friend
Down: 2=crossing guard; 3=mail carrier; 6=teacher; 7=classmate; 9=doctor